COMPSOGNATHUS

THE SMALLEST DINOSAUR

by

Elizabeth J. Sandell

DINOSAUR DISCOVERY ERA

Bancroft-Sage Publishing

601 Elkcam Circle, Suite C-7, Box 355, Marco, FL 33969

Exclusive distributor

Britannica
ENCYCLOPAEDIA BRITANNICA EDUCATIONAL CORPORATION

TRAINING & DEVELOPMENT

310 South Michigan Avenue Chicago, IL 60604

LIBRARY OF CONGRESS CATALOGING IN PUBLICATION DATA

Sandell, Elizabeth J.
  Compsognathus: the smallest dinosaur.

  (Dinosaur discovery era)
  SUMMARY: Describes Compsognathus, the dinosaur that was only the size of a modern chicken, and the prehistoric world of dinosaurs in general.
  1. Compsognathus--Juvenile literature. (1. Compsognathus. 2. Dinosaurs.) I. Oelerich, Marjorie L. II. Hansen, Harlan S. III. Vista III Design. IV. Title. V. Series.
QE862.S3S347   1989   567.9'7   88-39801
ISBN 0-944280-14-5 (lib. bdg.)
ISBN 0-944280-20-X (pbk bdg.)

International Standard Book Number:	Library of Congress Catalog Card Number:
Library Binding 0-944280-14-5	88-39801
Paperback Binding 0-944280-20-X	

SPECIAL THANKS FOR THEIR HELP AND COOPERATION TO:
Mary R. Carman, Paleontology Collection Manager
Field Museum of Natural History
Chicago, IL

John H. Ostrom, Ph.D., Professor of Geology
Peabody Museum of Natural History, Yale University
New Haven, CT

COMPSOGNATHUS

THE SMALLEST DINOSAUR

AUTHOR

Elizabeth J. Sandell

dedicated to Zachary Carman

EDITED BY

Marjorie L. Oelerich, Ph.D.
Professor of Early Childhood and Elementary Education
Mankato State University
Mankato, MN

Harlan S. Hansen, Ph.D.
Professor of Early Childhood and Elementary Education
University of Minnesota
Minneapolis, MN

ILLUSTRATED BY

Vista III Design

BANCROFT-SAGE PUBLISHING
533 8th St. So., Box 664, Naples, FL 33939-0664 USA

3

INTRODUCTION:
VISITING THE MUSEUM

"Now we're really going to find out about dinosaurs!" exclaimed Rosa, as she and her friends waited in the museum.

On this Saturday, they had come to the museum for a special program on dinosaurs. There would be a film which would tell about the life of dinosaurs and what might have caused all the dinosaurs to die.

As they were walking to their seats in the theater, Rosa and her friends passed models of two animals. One was very big — it reached almost to the ceiling. It looked like a dinosaur. The other one was very small. It did not look like a dinosaur.

"That dinosaur is very large! It looks scary!" exclaimed Mai Lee, as she walked past the big animal.

"I'm not scared, because I know that dinosaurs are extinct," said Matthew.

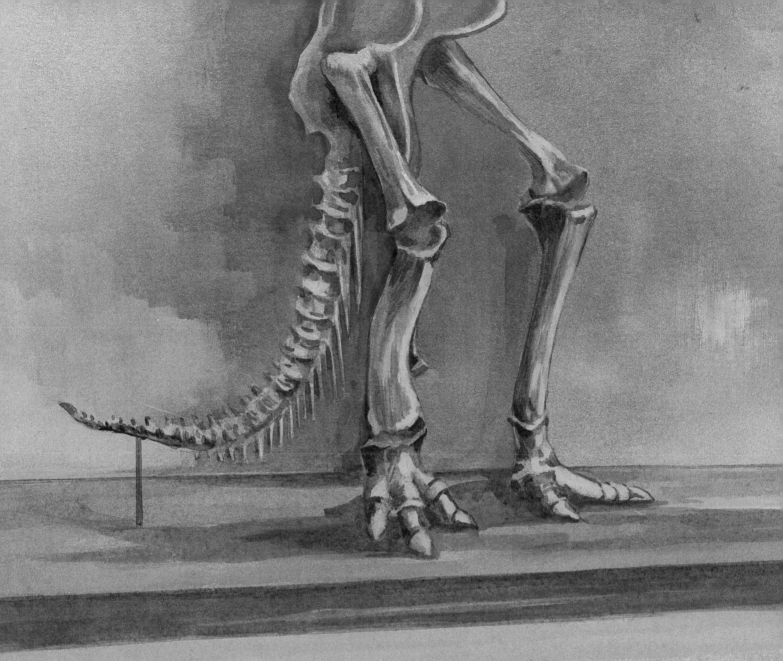

"That's right," agreed Rosa. "They were alive a long time ago, but no person living now has ever seen a live one. There are no more dinosaurs."

As the children sat down, the program began. Dr. Sanford, a paleontologist, introduced the film.

"Did you notice the models of two dinosaurs in the hall?" Dr. Sanford began. "One of them is very big and is named *Allosaurus.* The other dinosaur is quite small. It is called *Compsognathus.*"

The children looked at each other with surprise. That small animal was a dinosaur! It was no larger than a chicken!

"Let's start the film now to learn more about dinosaurs," Dr. Sanford said. "We will hear information about the life and death of this small dinosaur, *Compsognathus.*"

The group watched the film, "Life and Death of the Dinosaurs."

This film showed about different kinds of dinosaurs. It told about fossils which are found by scientists. Also, the film had information about how dinosaurs disappeared from the earth.

CHAPTER 1:
WHAT WERE DINOSAURS?

Dinosaur means "terrible lizard." This name is made from two Greek words. **Deinos** means "terrible," because scientists used to believe that all dinosaurs were very huge. **Sauros** means "lizard," because it was believed that dinosaurs were lizards. However, today, scientists know that dinosaurs were not lizards.

DIAPSIDS

Scientists have put dinosaurs in a group of animals called *diapsid*. This name comes from the Greek word **di,** which means "two," and the word **apsid,** which means "arch." There were two bony arches in the skull behind the eyes of these *diapsids*.

There are two groups of *diapsids*. Dinosaurs are in one group, which is called *archosaur* (ark´ uh sor´). Snakes and lizards, with which we are familiar, are in the other group. This group is named *lepidosaur* (le pid´ uh sor´).

Allosaurus

FAMILY TREE

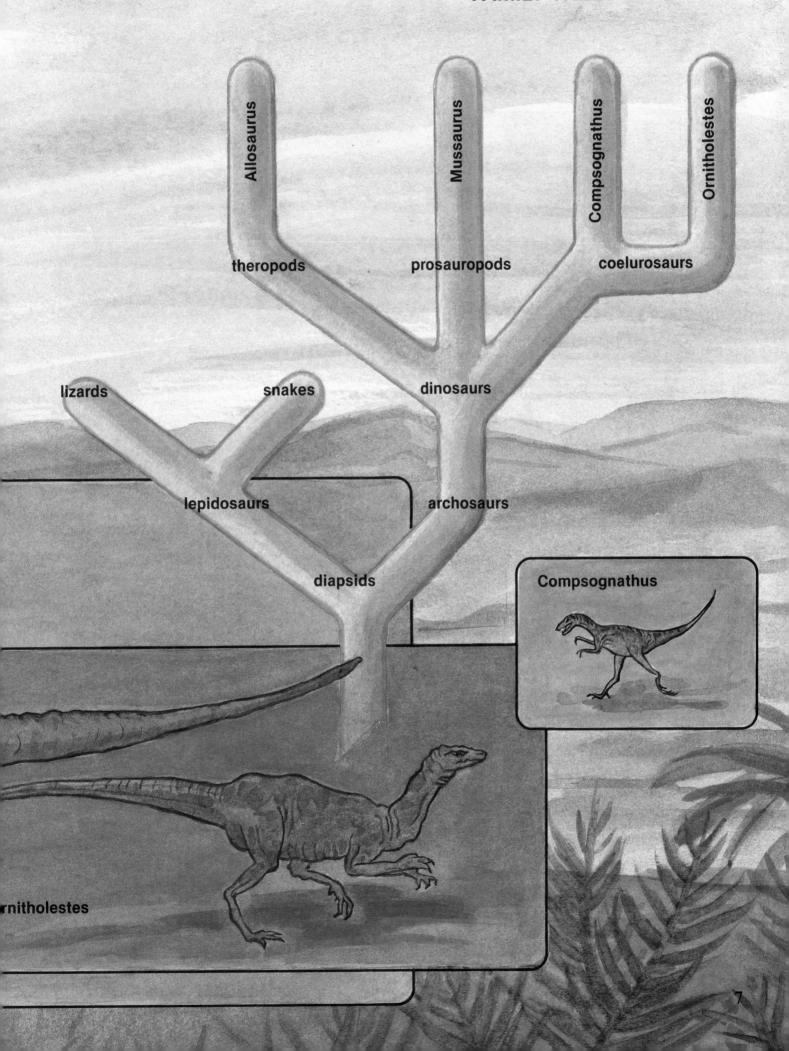

Allosaurus

Mussaurus

Compsognathus

Ornitholestes

theropods

prosauropods

coelurosaurs

lizards

snakes

dinosaurs

lepidosaurs

archosaurs

diapsids

Compsognathus

Ornitholestes

CHAPTER 2:
THE SMALLEST DINOSAUR

Some dinosaurs were as long as two or three city buses. Other dinosaurs were much smaller than that.

Fossils of some very small dinosaurs have been found by paleontologists. One tiny dinosaur skeleton was found in Argentina (South America) in 1971. Dr. José Bonaparte named this dinosaur *Mussaurus* (moos sor´ us), which means "mouse lizard." It was so small that it could be held in a person's hand. Perhaps, too, this was not a small adult dinosaur, but only a baby dinosaur that would be much bigger when it was fully grown.

Although *Compsognathus* (komp´ so nay´ thus) was not as small as *Mussaurus,* it is one of the smallest known dinosaurs. Its name means "elegant jaw," from the Greek words **kompos**, which means "elegant" or "pretty," and **gnathos**, which means "jaw."

THE LITTLE COELUROSAURS

Compsognathus was a dinosaur from the group of *archosaurs* which are known as *coelurosaur* (so luhr´ uh sor´). This name is from two Greek words. **Koilos** means "hollow," because of the hollow bones in *coelurosaurs*. **Sauros** means "lizard," because these animals were thought to be lizards. Now we know, though, that *coelurosaurs* were not lizards.

All *coelurosaurs* were quite small. Some were as small as a chicken. Others were about the size of an ostrich.

Compsognathus was among the smallest of the *coelurosaurs*.

APPEARANCE

Compsognathus was about 2.5 to 4 feet (91 cm to 1.2 m) long. It weighed only about 4.5 pounds (2 kg), because its hollow, thin-walled bones were not very heavy.

It had a small, pointed head and a flexible neck. Its jaw had many teeth, each of which had sharp points.

Compsognathus had four legs. Each of the two hind legs were long, like the legs of birds. This dinosaur ran on these strong legs, with the tail held behind for balance. It could run quickly.

The two front legs were very short. Each front leg had two claw-like fingers. *Compsognathus* did not use these legs for running. It may have used them to catch insects, lizards, and other small animals for food.

MEAT-EATERS

Because of evidence found in one fossil of *Compsognathus,* scientists believe that this dinosaur ate meat. In this case, there was a skeleton of a smaller animal inside the fossil of *Compsognathus.* Scientists used to think that this smaller one was a baby *Compsognathus.* Now, scientists have found that this skeleton was from a small lizard which this dinosaur had eaten.

Because we know that lizards can move fast, scientists know that *Compsognathus* must have been able to run quickly, too. Also, this dinosaur must have had good eyesight in order to see these fast-moving lizards.

CHAPTER 3:
WHEN COMPSOGNATHUS LIVED

By studying fossils, paleontologists can learn a great deal about *Compsognathus*. Paleontologists are special scientists who study fossils to learn about plants and animals from thousands of years ago. These scientists also have ideas about what the world was like when *Compsognathus* lived.

VERY RARE FOSSILS

Scientists have found only two fossil skeletons of *Compsognathus*. The first skeleton was found in West Germany (Europe), by Dr. Oberndorfer in the late 1850's. The most complete *Compsognathus* skeleton, though, was found in layers of rock near Nice, in southern France, in 1972.

Fossils are the remains of plants and animals from a long time ago. Fossils could be bones, teeth, shells, eggs, or insects. Or fossils could be imprints of leaves, feathers, or footprints.

Sometimes, animals would die near water. The bodies might be covered with mud or sand. The skin and muscle tissue would decay, but the bones could be preserved. Water which contained minerals would wash through every part of the bones or teeth. Then, the minerals would slowly turn these body parts into fossils. After a long time, even the mud turned into hard rocks.

LAND AND WEATHER

During the time that *Compsognathus* lived on earth, the land was almost connected, like the land shown on this map.

JURASSIC

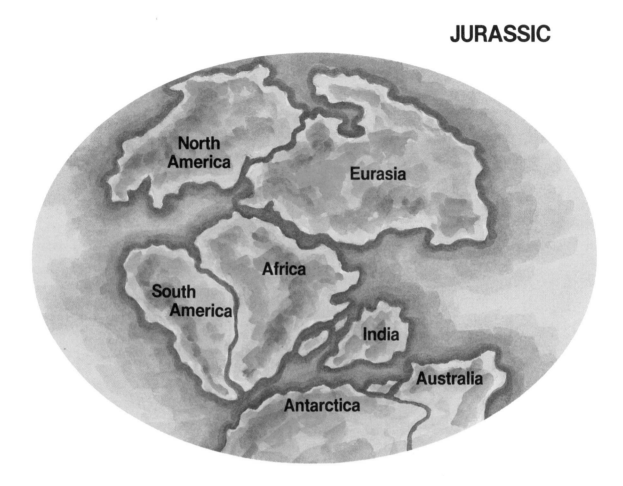

There were earthquakes and volcanoes, which caused the land to change as it moved up and down. Some land rose up high and became mountains. Other land became the bottom of rivers. Many rocks were pushed to the top of the earth. That is where scientists find fossils today.

The weather at that time may have been very mild. The summers were probably warm and wet. Perhaps there were no cold winters.

PLANTS AND INSECTS

Compsognathus ran through forests, which had many palm trees, ferns, Williamsonia, and other plants.

There were butterflies, dragonflies, and other insects. These insects probably bit *Compsognathus*, just like insects bother animals today. Perhaps *Compsognathus* would catch and eat some of these insects.

PROTECTION FROM ENEMIES

Compsognathus would try to stay out of the way of the dinosaurs that ate meat. Those dinosaurs would want to catch *Compsognathus* for food. If the big meat-eaters attacked *Compsognathus*, this little dinosaur could quickly change direction and run under low bushes to get away from the big animals.

Smaller, fast-moving enemies, like *Ornitholestes* (or nith o les´ teez), would hunt for *Compsognathus*. They were meat-eating dinosaurs, too, so they wanted to catch *Compsognathus* for food.

Ornitholestes was about 5 feet (1.5 m) long. Its name means "bird robber," because scientists used to believe that it caught birds to eat. Its name is from two Greek words. The word **ornithos,** which means "bird," was combined with **lestes,** which means "robber."

These dinosaurs, though, might not have been able to catch a fully-grown, healthy *Compsognathus*. Instead, they would need to find one that was very young, very old, or sick.

CHAPTER 4: DINOSAURS DISAPPEARED

What scientists do not know for sure is why the dinosaurs, including *Compsognathus*, disappeared. There are many different ideas about the death of dinosaurs.

One thought is that the earth was struck by a meteorite or an asteroid. Dust from this crash may have blocked out the sunlight and put the earth into cold darkness. Plants could no longer grow. Therefore, the dinosaurs that needed plants for food would have died. Then the meat-eaters would have died because there were not enough other animals for them to eat.

Another idea is that there were some new flowering plants that contained poisons which killed animals. However, many scientists do not believe that this would have caused all the dinosaurs to die.

Perhaps the movement of the land continents caused the sea level to drop. This would make great changes in the living conditions for dinosaurs. Perhaps dinosaurs could not live with these changes. Therefore, many of them would have died.

It is possible that there was less food after the land separated. This would mean the animals had to compete for food, which would result in starvation and death for some dinosaurs.

CONCLUSION:
MANY DIFFERENT IDEAS

"There is a great deal about dinosaurs that scientists do not know for sure," Dr. Sanford told Rosa and her friends after the film ended. "Scientists have many different ideas about how the dinosaurs lived and died. That's why we often say 'maybe,' 'perhaps,' 'scientists believe,' or 'possibly.'

"No one is sure how long it took all of the dinosaurs to die. It may have happened in a week, or it could have taken thousands of years," Dr. Sanford continued.

When Rosa arrived home, she told her family about the film. She talked about how dinosaurs might have lived and died.

"Dinosaurs lived many years ago," Rosa began. "Although some dinosaurs were very large, there were some that were quite small.

"We saw a film about a dinosaur which was about the size of a chicken. It is called *Compsognathus*.

TIME LINE

PERIOD

CHARACTERISTIC ANIMAL LIFE

AGE OF THE DINOSAURS

CRETACEOUS
65 MILLION YEARS TO
135 MILLION YEARS AGO

Triceratops
Pteranodon
Maiasaura
Tyrannosaurus rex
Plesiosaurus
Ankylosaurus

JURASSIC
136 MILLION YEARS TO
192 MILLION YEARS AGO

Apatosaurus
Allosaurus
Stegosaurus
Archaeopteryx
Compsognathus
Seismosaurus

TRIASSIC
193 MILLION YEARS TO
224 MILLION YEARS AGO

Mastodonsaurus
Rutiodon
Protosuchus
Plateosaurus

PERMIAN
225 MILLION YEARS TO
279 MILLION YEARS AGO

Eryops
Seymouria
Dimetrodon
Titanophoneus

CARBONIFEROUS
280 MILLION YEARS TO
345 MILLION YEARS AGO

Urocordylus
Hylonomus
Branchiosaurus

LIZARD (liz´ uhrd) is a kind of reptile. Most lizards are small with slender, scaly bodies; long tails; and four legs.

METEORITE (me´ te uh ryt) is a mass of stone or metal from outer space.

MINERALS (min´ uhr ulz) are parts of water, rocks, and land that are not plants or animals.

MUSEUM (myoo ze´ uhm) is a place for keeping and exhibiting works of nature and art, scientific objects, and other items.

MUSSAURUS (moos sor´ us) means "mouse lizard." The Latin word **mus** means "mouse," and the Greek word **sauros** means "lizard."

ORNITHOLESTES (or nith o les´ teez) means "bird robber." The Greek word **ornithos** means "bird," and **lestes** means "robber," because it was thought that this animal caught birds to eat. It was a coelurosaur which lived in North America.

PALEONTOLOGIST (pa´ le on tol´ uh jist) is a person who studies fossils to learn about plants and animals from thousands of years ago.

PROSAUROPODS (pro sor´ uh podz´) are one group of dinosaurs. Mussaurus belongs to this group.

REPTILES (rep´ tilz) are cold-blooded, egg-laying animals, such as snakes, alligators, and lizards. The legs grow out of the sides of their bodies, causing the reptiles to crawl rather than walk.

SCIENTIST (si´ uhn tist) is a person who studies objects or events.

SKELETON (skel´ uh tuhn) is the framework of bones of a body.

SKULL (skul) is the bony framework of the head of an animal.

THEROPODS (thir´ uh podz´) are one group of dinosaurs that ate meat and walked on their hind legs. Allosaurus is a member of this group.

THOUSAND (thou´ zuhnd) is ten times one hundred. It is shown as 1,000.

GLOSSARY

ALLOSAURUS (al´ uh sor´ us) means "other lizard" or "different lizard." The backbone of Allosaurus was different from that of all other dinosaurs.

ARCHOSAUR (ark´ uh sor´) is the name for one kind of dinosaur. When this name was first used, scientists thought that dinosaurs were lizards. Now, scientists know that dinosaurs were not lizards. However, the name "archosaur" is still used.

ASTEROID (as´ tuh roid) is a small planet in outer space.

COELUROSAUR (so luhr´ uh sor´) is the name of a group of dinosaurs. These dinosaurs had hollow bones. Now we know that coelurosaurs were not lizards.

COMPSOGNATHUS (komp´ so nay´ thus) is the name for one of the smallest known dinosaurs, which was only the size of a chicken. Compsognathus had hollow bones, a small and pointed head, sharp teeth, and a flexible neck. It moved very quickly on its two hind feet. Its hind legs were long, like the legs of birds. Each short, front leg had two claws. Fossils of Compsognathus were found in Germany and in France (Europe).

CYCAD (si´ kad) is a fern-like tree which lived many years ago.

DIAPSID (di ap´ sid) is one group of reptiles. These animals had two bony arches in the skull behind the eyes. There are two kinds of diapsids. Snakes and lizards are in one group. The other group includes the dinosaurs.

DINOSAUR (di´ nuh sor´) means "terrible lizard." The Greek word **deinos** means "terrible," and the word **sauros** means "lizard." Dinosaurs were not lizards.

EXTINCT (ek stingkt´) means no longer alive.

FOSSILS (fos´ uhlz) are the remains of plants and animals that lived years ago. The word **fossilis** means "something dug up."

LEPIDOSAUR (le pid´ uh sor´) is the group of diaspids which includes snakes and lizards. Dinosaurs were not lepidosaurs.

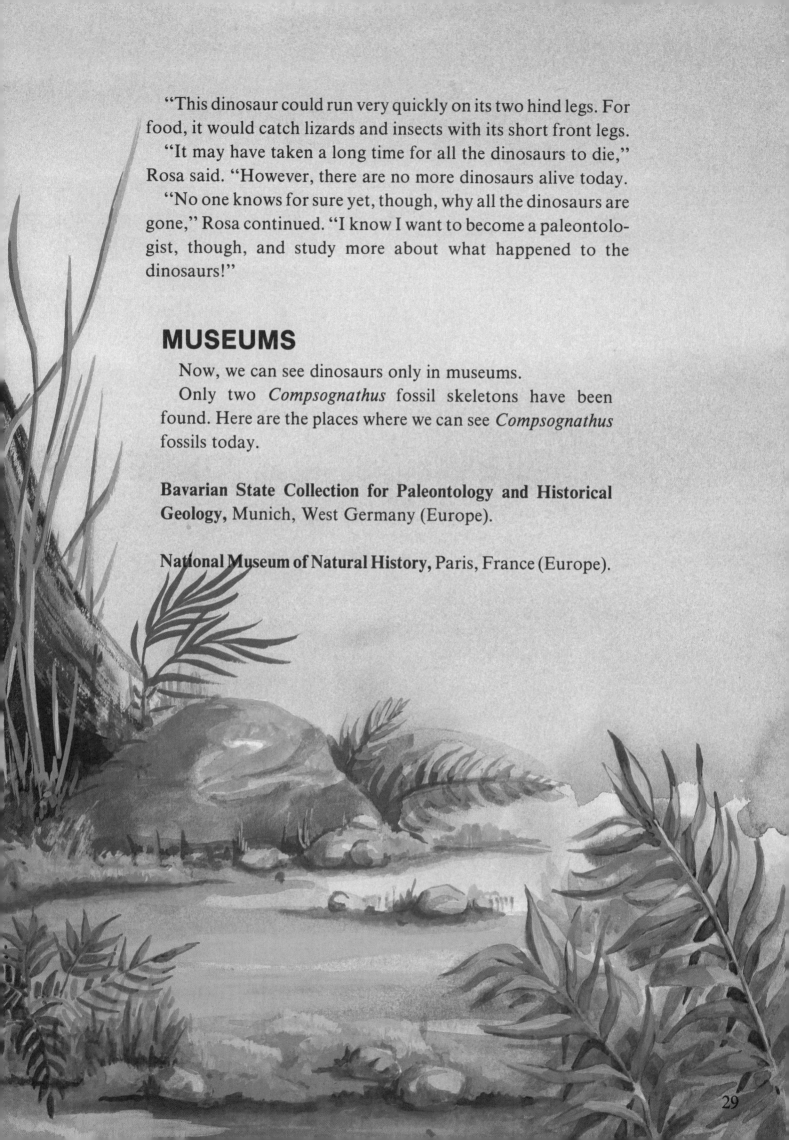

"This dinosaur could run very quickly on its two hind legs. For food, it would catch lizards and insects with its short front legs.

"It may have taken a long time for all the dinosaurs to die," Rosa said. "However, there are no more dinosaurs alive today.

"No one knows for sure yet, though, why all the dinosaurs are gone," Rosa continued. "I know I want to become a paleontologist, though, and study more about what happened to the dinosaurs!"

MUSEUMS

Now, we can see dinosaurs only in museums.

Only two *Compsognathus* fossil skeletons have been found. Here are the places where we can see *Compsognathus* fossils today.

Bavarian State Collection for Paleontology and Historical Geology, Munich, West Germany (Europe).

National Museum of Natural History, Paris, France (Europe).